Cool Hotels

teNeues

Editor:

Paco Asensio

Editorial coordination and text:

Ana Cristina G. Cañizares

English copyediting:

Juliet King

German translation:

Haike Falkenberg / Inken Wolthaus

French translation:

Michel Ficerai

Art direction:

Mireia Casanovas Soley

Graphic design / Layout:

Pilar Cano

Published in the US and Canada by
teNeues Publishing Company
16 West 22nd Street, New York, N.Y. 10010, USA
Tel.: 001-212-627-9090, Fax: 001-212-627-9511

Published in Germany, Austria and Switzerland by
teNeues Book Division
Kaistraße 18, 40211 Düsseldorf
Tel. 0049-(0)211-994597-0, Fax. 0049-(0)211-994597-40

Published in the UK and Ireland by
teNeues Publishing UK Ltd.
P.O. Box 402
West Byfleet, KT14 7ZF
Great Britain
Tel. 0044-1932-403509, Fax. 0044-1932-403514

www.teneues.com

Editorial project:

© 2001 **LOFT** publications
Via Laietana, 32, 4º Of. 92
08003 Barcelona. Spain
Tel.: +34 93 268 80 88
Fax: +34 93 268 70 73
e-mail: loft@loftpublications.com
www.loftpublications.com

Printed by:

Anman Gràfiques del Vallés
Sabadell, Spain

March 2003

Die Deutsche Bibliothek - CIP-Einheitsaufnahme
Ein Titeldatensatz für diese Publikation ist bei der
Deutschen Bibliothek erhältlich.

ISBN: 3-8238-5556-5

© Undine Pröhl

© Undine Pröhl

Choosing a place to stay abroad, whether it be for business or pleasure, has become an important factor in the itinerary of most of today´s travelers. A hotel is no longer just a temporary lodging space with the sole purpose of spending the night. It has become the embodiment of defined lifestyles, representing a certain kind of client with an established set of tastes and standards.

Luxury is considered in terms of quality versus quantity. People look for a place where they can feel at home and relish perks they may not have otherwise. They take pleasure in an environment they consider to be beautiful and unique. The level of importance placed on quality of style is clearly reflected in every one of the hotels featured in COOL HOTELS. Designed by some of the world´s most renown architects and designers, these hotels demonstrate their worth through all kinds of detail. Some cater to the jet-setting businessperson, others to adventure-seekers, and others to those who simply search for a peaceful respite. Whether more classical than futuristic, or more modern than rustic, they all share a pure, contemporary vision.

On an ever shrinking planet, travel is as frequent as dialing a phone number. Thanks to hotels like these, we can rest assured that our journeys will be punctuated by perfect places offering us much more than just a good night´s sleep.

Die Wahl des Aufenthaltsortes in der Ferne, ob aus geschäftlichem Anlass oder zum Vergnügen, ist heute für die meisten Reisenden zu einem der wichtigsten Aspekte der Reiseplanung geworden. Ein Hotel ist nicht mehr nur eine zeitlich begrenzte Station mit dem einzigen Zweck, die Nacht zu verbringen, sondern es verkörpert klar definierte Lebensstile, indem es eine bestimmte Klientel mit ihren etablierten Vorlieben und Standards repräsentiert. Luxus wird in Qualität, nicht in Quantität gemessen. Die Menschen suchen nach einem Rückzugsort, an dem sie sich dennoch zu Hause fühlen, wo sie Extras genießen können, die sie sonst vielleicht nicht so einfach haben, und um in einer Umgebung zu schwelgen, die sie schön und einzigartig finden.

Die große Bedeutung, die der Qualität des Stils zukommt, wird von jedem einzelnen der in diesem Band vorgestellten Hotels deutlich zur Schau gestellt. Gestaltet von den bekanntesten Architekten und Designern weltweit, bekunden diese Hotels ihren Wert durch die verschiedensten Details. Einige sind auf jetsettende Geschäftsleute, andere auf Abenteuerlustige und wieder andere auf diejenigen zugeschnitten, die einfach nur eine friedliche Ruhepause suchen. Ob eher klassisch oder lieber exzentrisch, eher modern oder lieber rustikal, allen ist eine absolut zeitgenössische Vision gemeinsam.

Auf unserem ständig kleiner werdenden Planeten ist Reisen so alltäglich geworden wie eine Telefonnummer zu wählen. Dank dieser Hotels können wir sicher sein, dass unsere Reisen an Plätzen Halt machen, die viel mehr als nur eine angenehme Nacht bieten.

© Undine Pröhl

© Undine Pröhl

Le choix d'un lieu de séjour à l'étranger, pour les affaires ou pour le plaisir, est devenu un facteur crucial dans les plans de voyage de la plupart des voyageurs contemporains. Un hôtel n'est plus seulement un espace d'hébergement temporaire, avec pour seule finalité de passer la nuit. Il incarne désormais des styles de vie précis, symboles d'un certain type de client avec des goûts et des valeurs clairement définis. Le luxe est une affaire de qualité, non de quantité. Chacun cherche un endroit pour s'échapper tout en se sentant chez soi, pour se délecter de plaisirs inaccessibles autrement et pour jouir d'un environnement perçu comme merveilleux et unique.

L'importance de la qualité stylistique est clairement réfléchie par chacun des hôtels décrit dans **COOL HOTELS**. Conçus par quelques-uns des designers et architectes les plus en vue, ces hôtels affichent leur valeur dans chaque petit détail. Certains s'adressent aux hommes d'affaires de la Jet Set, d'autres aux aventuriers et d'autres, enfin, à ceux recherchant un havre de paix. Classique ou excentrique, moderne ou rustique, tous partagent une vision essentiellement contemporaine.

Sur une planète toujours plus exiguë, voyager est devenu aussi fréquent qu'un appel téléphonique. Grâce à ces hôtels, nous pouvons être sûrs que nos voyages seront ponctués d'endroits parfaits, offrant bien plus qu'une nuit de sommeil.

© Undine Pröhl

9

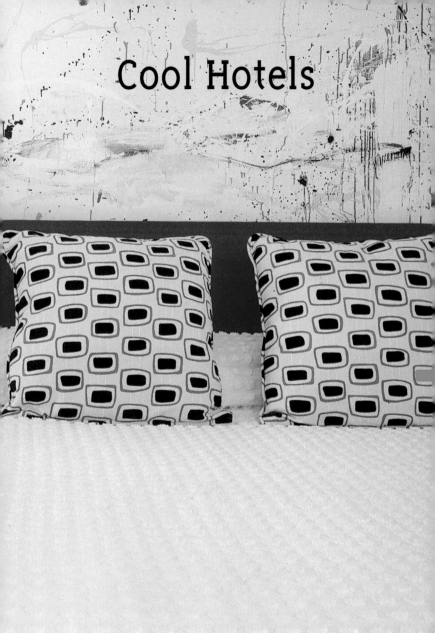

Cool Hotels

The Royal Hotel

Architect: Jordan Mozer

Photographer: © Pep Escoda

Original construction date: 1938

Original architect: Henry Hohauser and L. Murray Dixon

Address: 758 Washington Avenue, Miami Beach, FL 33139, US

tel. 1 305 673 9009 fax 1 305 673 9244

www.royalhotelsouthbeach.com

Opening date: November 2000

Rooms: 42

Services: restaurant, bar, business facilities, press, temperature control, laundry service, minibar, complementary continental breakfast

Ace Hotel

Architect: Eric Hentz Mallet

Photographer: © Jim Henkens, © Chad Brow

Owners: Doug Herrick, Alex Calderwood, Wade Weigel

Address: 2423 1st Avenue, Seattle, WA 98121, US

tel. 1 206 448 4721 fax 1 206 374 0745

reservations@theacehotel.com

Opening date: 1999

Rooms: 34

Services: restaurant, modem lines, satellite, air conditioning, minibar, hair salon, laundry service, day care center, non-smoking rooms, parking, animals permitted

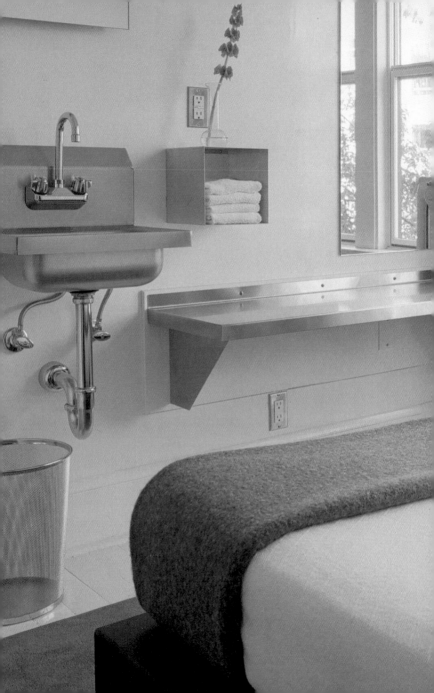

Maison 140

Architects: Tolkin & Associates

Interior designers: Kelly Wearstler Interior Design (KWID)

Photographer: © Undine Pröhl

Owner: Elkor Realty Corporation

Address: 140 South Lasky Drive, Beverly Hills, CA 90212, US

tel. 1 310 281 4000 fax 1 310 281 4001

www.maison140.com

Original construction: 1930

Opening date: August 2000

Rooms: 45

Services: restaurant, bar, gym, conference rooms, laundry service, swimming pool, car rental, cable, radio, CD player/cassette, Internet access, minibar, parking

W Los Angeles

Architect: Jon Brouse

Interior designers: Dayna Lee, Power Strip in alliance with Starwood Design Group

Photographer: © Undine Pröhl

Owners: Starwood Hotels & Resorts WorldWide, Inc.

Address: 930 Hilgard Avenue, Los Angeles, CA 90024, US

tel. 1 310 208 8765 fax 1 310 824 0355

www.whotels.com

Opening date: December 2000

Rooms: 258

Services: Mojo restaurant, bar; health and beauty salon (swedish massage, aromatherapy,

shiatsu, reflexology, facial and body treatments), gym, conference rooms, audiovisual equipment,

CD player; radio, video, scanner; fax, printer; parking

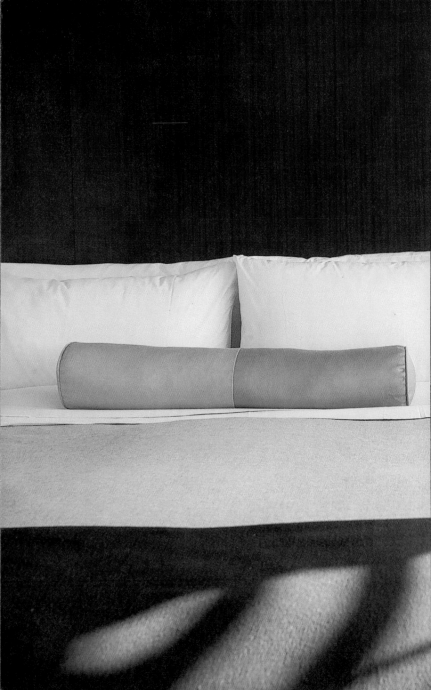

Avalon Hotel

Architect: Koning Eizenberg

Interior designer: Kelly Wearstler

Photographer: © Undine Pröhl

Owner: Elkor Realty Group

Address: 9400 West Olympic Boulevard, Beverly Hills, CA 90212, US

tel. 1 310 277 5221   fax 1 310 277 4928

www.avalon-hotel.com

Original construction: 1949

Opening date: 1999

Rooms: 88

Services: restaurant, bar, health and beauty salon, gym, swimming pool and private cabins, mobile phone, car and limousine rentals, fax, CD player, 24 hr room service

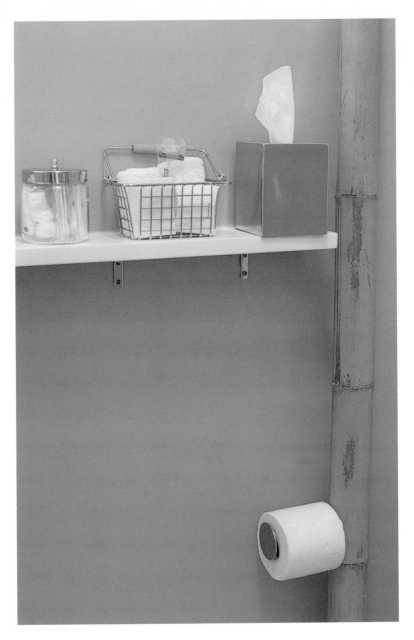

WNY Union Square

Architect/designer: David Rockwell

Photographer: © Jordi Miralles

Address: 201 Park Avenue South, New York, NY 10003, US

tel. 1 212 253 9119 fax 1 212 253 9229

www.whotels.com

Opening date: December 1998

Rooms: 722

Services: restaurant, bar, gym, library, high tech business facilities, high speed connections, 24 hr room service

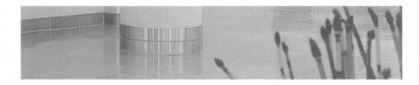

Sunset Marquis

Designers: Oliva Villaluz & Barry Salehian

Photographer: © Undine Pröhl

Owner: George Rosenthal

Original construction: 1936

Furniture by: Villaluz & Salehian

Address: 7005 Melrose Avenue, Los Angeles, CA 90038, US

tel. 1 323 658 8700 fax 1 323 658 8750

reservations@sunsetmarquishotel.com

www.sunsetmarquishotel.com

Opening date: 2001

Rooms: 108, 12 villas

Services: restaurant, bar, sauna, press, recording studio, butler service

The glass entry facade admits unfettered light to fill the reception area, where solidly proportioned furnishings commit the space to human scale.

Die gläserne Eingangsfassade gibt dem Tageslicht ungehindert den Weg frei in den Rezeptionsbereich, wo solid proportionierte Möbelstücke den Raum auf einen menschlichen Maßstab bringen.

La façade en verre laisse passer librement une lumière emplissant toute la réception, dont lemobilier strictement proportionné réduit l'espace à des dimensions humaines.

Dylan Hotel

Architect: M. Castedo

Interior designer: Jeffrey Beers International

Photographer: © Jordi Miralles

Address: 52 East 41 Street, New York, NY 10017, US

tel. 1 212 338 0500   fax 1 212 338 0569

www.dylanhotel.com

info@dylanhotel.com

Original construction: 19th Century

Rooms: 108

Services: restaurant, bar, TV, dataport, gym, non-smoking floors

Bentley

Architect/designer: Goodman Charlton Inc.

Photographer: © Michael Kleinberg

Address: 500 East 62nd Street, New York, NY 10021, US

tel. 1 212 644 6000 fax 1 212 759 5023

www.nychotels.com

Opening date: April 1998

Rooms: 197

Services: rooftop lounge and restaurant, complimentary cappucino bar, library, concierge,

on demand movies, data port, room service, 24 hr parking

A rectangular panel frames a beautiful tube vase of delicate flowers, illuminated from behind. A uniform chromatic palette of greys, cremes, beiges and browns accompany contemporary designer furniture. The library features a mixture of styles, conceding an intimate and eclectic atmosphere.

Eine rechteckige Konsole rahmt eine feine schlanke Vase mit zarten Blumen ein, sie wird von hinten beleuchtet. Die einheitliche Farbpalette aus Grautönen, Creme, Beige und Braun ergänzt die zeitgenössischen Designermöbel. Die Bibliothek im Stilmix vermittelt eine zurückgezogene und eklektische Atmosphäre.

Un panneau rectangulaire encadre un remarquable vase de fleurs délicates, illuminé par l'arrière. Une palette chromatique uniforme de gris, crèmes, beiges et bruns accompagne un mobilier de créateur contemporain. La bibliothèque affiche un mélange de styles, avouant une atmosphère intime et éclectique.

Chelsea Hotel

Architect: Alan Lieberman

Photographer: © Pep Escoda

Owner: Alan Lieberman

Address: 9944 Washington Avenue, Soutbeach, FL 33139, US

tel. 1 305 534 4069   fax 1 305 672 6712

www.thehotelchelsea.com

Original construction: 1936

Opening date: January 2001

Rooms: 42

Services: restaurant, bar, massage, gym passes, VIP passes to all the local clubs, cable, CD player, Internet access, minibar, parking

The Hotel

Architect: L. Murray Dixon

Interior designer: Todd Oldham

Photographer: © Pep Escoda

Owner: Goldman Properties

Address: 801 Collins Avenue, Miami Beach, FL 33139, US

tel. 1 305 531 2222 fax 1 305 531 3222

info@thehotelofsouthbeach.com

www.thehotelofsouthbeach.com

Original construction: 1939

Opening date: November 1998

Rooms: 52

Services: wish restaurant, health and beauty salon, gym, Internet access, CD player, business center,

audiovisual equipment, exterior pool with bar service, gift shop, minibar, parking

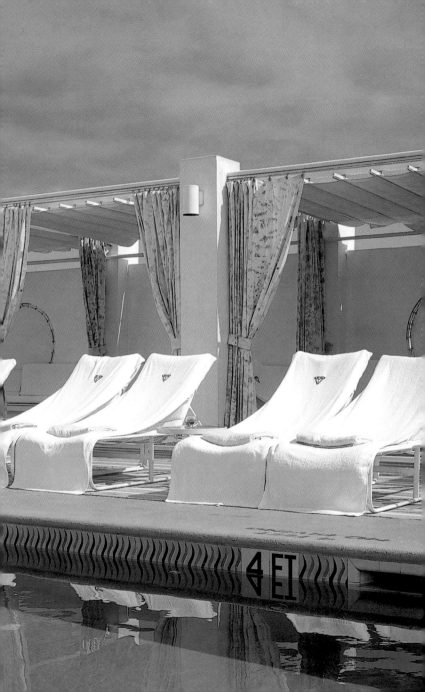

Orbit In

Architect: Lance O´Donnell (Escalante Architects)

Photographer: © Undine Pröhl

Designer: Herb W. Burns

Owner: The Lathom Group/Tim Ellis

Address: 562 W. Arenas, Palm Springs, CA 92262, US

tel. I 760 323 3585   fax I 760 323 3599

www.orbitin.com

mail@orbitin.com

Rooms: 10

Services: restaurant, bar, air conditioning, CD, TV/VCR, data ports, video library,

private patios, minibar

Whitelaw

Designer: Alan Lieberman

Photographer: © Pep Escoda

Original construction date: 1936

Original architect: Albert Anis

Address: 808 Collins Avenue, South Beach, FL 33139, US

tel. 1 305 398 7000 fax 1 305 398 7010

www.whitelawhotel.com

Opening date: January 2000

Rooms: 49

Services: restaurant, bar, fax, internet, business facilities, laundry service

Delano Hotel

Architects: PMG Architects - Peter Grumpel, Jury Álvarez

Interior designer: Philippe Starck

Owner: Beach Hotel Associates

Photographer: © Pep Escoda

Original construction date: 1947

Address: 1685 Collins Avenue, Miami Beach, FL 33139, US

tel. 1 305 672 2000   fax 1 305 532 0099   (NY, Miami, LA)

Opening date: June 1995

Rooms: 208

Services: restaurant, bar, business facilities, laundry service, voicemail

Hudson Rocks

Designer: Philippe Starck

Photographer: © Jordi Miralles

Owner: Ian Schrager

Address: 356 West 58 Street, New York, NY 10019, US

tel. 1 212 554 6000   fax 1 212 554 6001

www.ianschragerhotels.com

Original construction: 1928

Opening date: October 2000

Rooms: 1,000

Services: cafeteria, health and beauty salon, gym, audiovisual equipment, banquet and
convention rooms, library, private garden

Century Hotel

Designer: Brian Stoner

Photographer: © Pep Escoda

Address: 140 Ocean Drive, Miami Beach, FL 33139, US

        tel. I 305 674 8855 fax I 305 538 5733

        www.centuryhotelsobe.com

Original construction date: 1939

Original architect: Henry Hohauser

Opening date: November 2000

Rooms: 31

Services: restaurant, bar, high tech business facilities, gym, dryer, video deck, minibar,

        voicemail, 24 hr room service

The Cincinnatian Hotel

Architect: Samuel Hannaford

Photographer: © Don Ventre

Address: 601 Vine Street, Cincinnati, Ohio 45202, US

tel. 1 513 381 3000 fax 1 513 381 2659

www.cincinnatianhotel.com

info@cincinnatianhotel.com

Opening date: 1987

Rooms: 146

Services: restaurant, bar, business facilities, dual shower, health spa, 24 hr room service

Fifteen Beacon

Interior designer: Celeste Cooper

Photographer: © Richard Mandelkorn

Original construction: 1722

Address: 15 Beacon Street, Boston, Massachussetts 02108, US

tel. 1 617 670 1500   fax 1 617 670 2525

www.15beacon.com

hotel@xvbeacon.com

Opening date: 2000

Rooms: 61

Services: restaurant, bar, business facilities, high speed connections,
cordless phone, satellite, minibar

The Hempel

Architect: Anouska Hempel

Photographer: © Gunnar Knechtel

Owner: Fujita UK Ltd.

Address: 31-35 Craven Hill Gardens, London W2 3EA, UK

tel. 44 20 7298 9000 fax 44 20 74 02 4666

www.the-hempelhotel.com

hotel@the-hempel.co.uk

Original construction: 19th Century

Opening date: July 1996

Rooms: 41 rooms, 8 apartments

Services: bar, restaurant I-Thai, private dining room, conference room, library, garden
for cocktail and reception parties, two telefone lines, fax and modem lines,
CD player, video, air conditioning, minibar, television, 24 hr room service

The design of each room is distinct, making them individual and unique.
A living area usually lies in front of the bed, which may have a canopy or simply
rest on the floor. Occasional Chinese pieces create a fantastic contrast to the
predominant shades of white, black, and beige.

Das Design jeden Raumes ist unterschiedlich und macht ihn individuell und einmalig. Vor dem Bett, das
unter einem Baldachin oder einfach auf dem Boden steht, erstreckt sich der Aufenthaltsraum. Vereinzelte
chinesische Objekte bilden einen fantastischen Kontrast zu den vorherrschenden Schattierungen in Weiß,
Schwarz und Beige.

Le design différent de chaque pièce les rend uniques. Une aire de séjour s'étend habituellement devant le
lit, pouvant être revêtu d'un dais, ou reposer directement sur le sol. Ça et là des oeuvres chinoises créent
un contraste original avec les ombres de blanc, de noir et de beige, omniprésentes.

Saint Martin's Lane

Designer: Philippe Starck

Photographer: © Todd Eberle

Owner: Ian Schrager

Address: 45 St. Martins Lane, London WC2N 4HX, UK

tel. 44 207 300 5500   fax 44 207 300 5501

www.ianschragerhotels.com

Original construction: 1960

Opening date: September 1999

Rooms: 204

Services: gourmet restaurant, bar, 24 hr concierge, gym, international news, gift shop,

multimedia, entertainment theatre

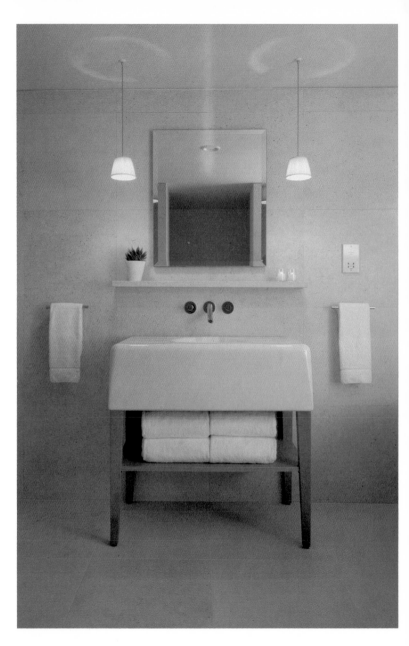

Sanderson Hotel

Architect: Philippe Starck

Photographer: © Mihail Moldoveanu, © Todd Eberle

Owner: Ian Schrager

Address: 50, Berners Street, London W1T 3NG, UK

tel. 44 207 300 1400 fax 44 207 300 1401

www.ianschragerhotels.com

reservations@sanderson.schragerhotels.com

Original construction: late 1950´s

Opening date: April 2000

Rooms: 150

Services: Spoon restaurant, Long Bar and Purple Bar, health center (diets, massage, yoga, gym), day care center, conference rooms, gift shop, CD player, cable, vídeo, DVD library with over 1,500 films, radio via satelite, private gym, 24 hr room service, parking

Great Eastern Hotel

Architects: Manser Associates

Interior/graphic designer: Conran Design

Photographer: © Peter Cook, © Jean Cazals, © James Merell, © Tim Winter

Owner: Conran Holdings & Wyndham International

Address: Liverpool St., London EC2M 7QN, UK

tel. 44 207 618 5000 fax 44 207 618 5001

www.great-eastern-hotel.co.uk

sales@great-eastern-hotel.co.uk

Opening date: February 2000

Rooms: 267

Services: restaurant, bar, gym, laundry, aromatherapy, minibar, business facilities, valet parking

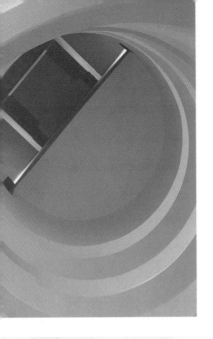

Once one of the grand hotels of the golden age of railway travel, its new design features the introduction of modern design alongside the revival of the classic. No two bedrooms are alike, the lower floors more elegant and the higher floors light and fresh.

Einst eines der großen Hotels des goldenen Zeitalters der Bahnreisen, vereint die Neugestaltung heute modernes Design mit wieder aufgelebten Klassikern. Kein Zimmer gleicht dem anderen: die unteren Etagen sind eher elegant, die oberen Stockwerke hell und frisch gehalten.

Autrefois l'un des grands hôtels de l'âge d'or du chemin de fer, son nouveau design voit l'apparition du modernisme accompagner la renaissance du classicisme. Aucune chambre n'est identique, les niveaux inférieurs plus élégants et les niveaux supérieurs frais et légers.

The Westbourne Hotel

Architect: MacConvilles

Interior designer: CAI

Project co-ordinator: Giles Baker

Photographer: © Gunnar Knechtel

Address: 163-165 Westbourne Grove, London W11 2RS, UK

      tel. 44 207 243 6008 fax 44 207 229 7204

Opening date: September 2000

Rooms: 20

Services: restaurant, bar, business facilities, DVD, laundry service, artworks

One Aldwych

Designers: Gordon Campbell Gray & Mary Fox Linton

Photographer: © Gunnar Knechtel

Original construction: 1907

Original architect: Mewes & Davis

Address: 1 Aldwych, London WC2B 4BZ, UK

tel. 44 207 300 1000   fax 44 207 300 1001

www.onealdwych.co.uk

sales@onealdwych.co.uk

Opening date: July 1998

Rooms: 105

Services: restaurant, bar, individual air conditioning, satellite, valet parking,

laundry service, minibar, 24 hr room service

...riors are contemporary, elegant, and comfortable, ...h a touch of classicism. The hotel houses a collection ...contemporary art, about 350 works in total.

... Innenausstattung ist modern, elegant und ...nfortabel - mit einem Hauch Klassizismus. Eine ...stsammlung aus insgesamt rund 350 Werken ...d über das gesamte Haus verteilt ausgestellt.

... intérieurs sont contemporains, élégants et ...fortables, avec une note de classicisme. L'hôtel ...te une collection d'art moderne, de près de ... pièces.

My Hotel

Architects: Conran Design (Terence Conran)

Photographer: © Gunnar Knechtel

Owner: Andy Thrasivoulou

Address: 11-13 Bayley Street, Bedford Square, London WC1B 3HD, UK

tel. 44 20 7667 6000   fax 44 20 7667 6044/7667 6001

www.myhotels.co.uk

Opening date: March 1999

Rooms: 68

Services: bar, restaurant, health and beauty salon (sauna, jacuzzi, massage), gym,
day care center, shops, casino, conference rooms, library, solarium, cable,
Internet access, 24 hr room service

Side Hotel

Architects: Störmer Architekten

Interior designer: Matteo Thun

Photographer: © Gunnar Knechtel

Owner: The Seaside Group

Address: Drehbahn, 49, 20354 Hamburg, Germany

tel. 49 40 30 99 90   fax 49 40 30 99 93

info@side-hamburg.de

www.side-hamburg.de

Opening date: April 2001

Rooms: 178

Services: bar, restaurant, gym, massage, jacuzzi, banquet and conference rooms, audiovisual equipment, swimming pool, two telefone lines, fax and modem

Red is the color used for much of the decor, paired up with dark wood, white ceilings, and bright lighting. Straight lines predominate in the bar while the unique lounge is a dreamy world of round and curved objects. Bright citrus tones against a crisp white background create a fresh modern feel.

Rot ist die vorherrschende Farbe der Dekoration, gepaart mit dunklem Holz, wißen Decken und strahlendem Licht. In der Bar dominieren gerade Linien, während die Lounge eine einmalige Traumwelt runder und geschwungener Objekte ist. Knackige Aitrustöne vor dem blendend weißen Hintergrund vermitteln eine frische, moderne Atmosphäre.

Le rouge, saisissant, est employé pour la plupart du décor, associé au bois sombre, aux plafonds blancs et à un éclairage lumineux. Les lignes droites prédominent dans le bar, l'unique salon étant un songe d'objects ronds et courbes. Les ton jaune lumineux, s'équilibrant avec l'arrière plan blanc vif, créent une sensation fraîche et moderne.

Gastwerk Hotel

Architect: Klaus Peter Lange

Interior designers: Regine Schwethelm & Sybille von Heyden

Photographer: © Andrea Flack, © Johannes Marburg, © Ute Schuckmann, © Michael Haydn

Original construction: 1898

Address: Beim Alten Gaswerk, 3 / Daimlerstr., 22761 Hamburg, Germany

tel. 49 40 890 62-0 fax 49 40 890 62-20

www.gastwerk-hotel.de

info@gastwerk-hotel.de

Opening date: January 2000

Rooms: 100

Services: restaurant, bar, business facilities, satellite, video, minibar

Hopper Hotel et cetera

Architects: Architekten HKR

Interior designers: Norbert Hentges, Rolf Kursawe, Petra Rehberg Thierdecke

Photographer: © Uwe Spoering

Address: Brüsseler Strasse 26, 50674 Köln, Germany

   tel. 49 221 92440 0 fax 49 221 92440 06

   www.hopper.de

   hotel@hopper.de

Opening date: January 1997

Rooms: 49

Services: restaurant, bar, cocktail bar, business facilities, gym, sauna

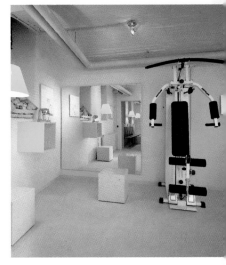

Wasserturm

Architects: Hopf-Group

Interior designer: Andree Putman

Original construction: 1868 - 1872

Address: Kaygasse 2, 50676 Köln, Germany

       tel. 49 221 20080   fax 49 221 200 8888

Opening date: 1990

Rooms: 88

Services: restaurant, bar, gym, sauna, solarium, chauffer service, 24 hr room service, free valet parking

Hotel Pergolese

Architect and interior designer: Réna Dumas

Photographer: © Pere Planells

Owner: Edith Vidalenc

Address: 3, rue Pergolèse, 75116 Paris, France

tel. 33 1 53 64 04 04 fax 33 1 53 64 04 40

www.hotelpergolese.com

hotel@pergolese.com

Original construction: 1900

Opening date: September 1991

Rooms: 40

Services: bar, restaurant, hair salon, gym, laundry service, fax, convention room with audiovisual equipment, parking, animales are permitted, cable and satellite, Internet access, minibar, air conditioning, 24 hr. room service

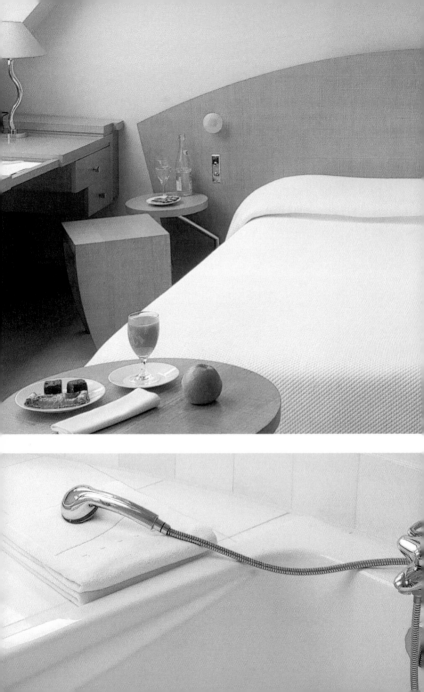

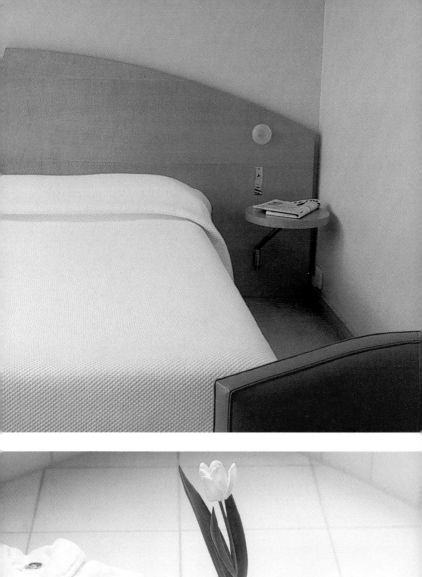

Bel Ami

Architect: Christian Lalande

Interior designers: Nathalie Battesti, Veronique Terreaux

Photographer: © Pere Planells

Owners: Westmont/Allince et Goldman Sachs

Address: 7-11, Rue St-Benoît, Saint-Germain-des-Prés, 75116 Paris, France

tel. 33 1 42 61 53 53 fax 33 1 49 27 09 33

www.hotel-bel-ami.com

contact@hotel-bel-ami.com

Original construction: late 19th Century

Opening date: January 2000

Rooms: 115 and 1 luxury suite

Services: bar La Cantina, laundry and drycleaners, conference room, room with TV screens, Internet access, library, cable, CD player, minibar, air conditioning

Hotel Square

Designer and owner: Patrick Derderian

Furniture: Philipe Hurel

Address: 3, Rue De Boulainvilliers, 75016 Paris, France

tel. 33 14 414 9190 fax 33 14 414 9199

www.hotelsquare.com

Opening date: June 1995

Rooms: 22

Services: restaurant, bar, business facilities, fax, voicemail, air conditioning,

laundry service, 24 hr room service

Hotel Montalembert

Designer: Grace Leo-Andrieu, François Chambsaur

Photographer: © Gilles Trillard

Original construction: 1926

Address: 3, Rue de Montalembert, 75007 Paris, France

tel. 33 1 4549 6868   fax 33 1 4549 6949

www.montalembert.com

Opening date: August 2000

Rooms: 56

Services: restaurant, bar, high tech connections, internet

The Lady's First Hotel

Architect: Pia Schmid

Photographer: © Miquel Tres

Owner: Frauenhotel AG

Address: Mainaustrasse 24, 8008 Zürich, Switzerland

        tel. 41 1 380 80 10 fax 41 1 380 80 20

        www.ladysfirst.ch

        info@ladysfirst.ch

Original construction: 19th Century

Opening date: 1999

Rooms: 28

Services: restaurant, health and beauty salon (sauna, baths, massage), solarium

The original ceiling height was maintained in the rooms. Minimal decoration keeps them uncluttered. Here, an intense red backdrop behind the bed contrasts with the cool tones offered by the bathroom´s glass, stone, and white mosaic.

Die ursprüngliche Deckenhöhe der Räume wurde beibehalten. Die minimale Einrichtung hält die Zimmer frei und ordentlich. Ein intensiv roter Hintergrund hinter dem Bett kontrastiert mit den kühlen Tönen der Badezimmereinrichtung: Glas, Stein und weiße Mosaike.

La hauteur de plafond originelle a été maintenue dans les chambres, la décoration minimale leur donnant un aspect aéré. Ici, une toile de fond rouge derrière le lit contraste avec les tons frais proposés par le verre, la pierre et la mosaïque blanche de la salle de bain.

Widder Hotel

Architect/designer: Tilla Theus

Photographer: © Miquel Tres

Address: Rennweg 7, 8001 Zurich, Switzerland

tel. 41 1 224 2526 fax 41 1 224 2424

www.widderhotel.ch

home@widderhotel.ch

Opening date: March 1995

Rooms: 49

Services: restaurant, bar, high-tech business facilities, gym, rooftop bathhouse/solarium/healthbar, gift shop, minibar, 24 hr room service, non-smoking rooms upon request

Bleiche Hotel

Architect: Huber David Ambrosius

Photographer: © Miquel Tres

Owner: Otto & John Honegger AG

Address: In der Bleiche, 8636 Wald, Switzerland

tel. 41 55 256 70 10 fax 41 55 256 70 21

www.bleiche.ch

bleiche@bleiche.ch

Original construction: 19th Century

Opening date: summer 2000

Rooms: 80

Services: bar, restaurant, dry cleaners, apartments, handicraft shops, art gallery, medical service, Internet access

Bar Hotel Seehof

Architects: Frei & Ehrensperger

Photographer: © Miquel Tres

Owners: Karin and Jurg Muller

Address: Seehofstrasse 11, 8008 Zurich, Switzerland

tel. 41 1 254 5757 fax 41 1 254 5758

www.hotelseehof.ch

reception@seehof.ch

Opening date: April 1999

Rooms: 19

Services: restaurant, bar, exhibitions, phone/fax/modem, minibar

These white cubes, furnished with dark wood shelves and the necessary bits, overlook a courtyard of pink and pistachio colored houses.

Diese weißen Würfel, mit dunklen Holzregalen und allen erforderlichen Elementen ausgestattet, haben Blick auf den Innenhof mit pink- und pistazienfarbenen Häusern.

Ces cubes blancs, meublés d'étagères en bois sombre et de menus objets, surplombent une cour peuplée de maisons aux couleurs rose et pistache.

Hotel Diplomatic

Architects: GCA Arquitectos

Photographer: © Jordi Miralles

Address: Pau Claris, 122, 08009 Barcelona, Spain

tel. 34 93 272 3810 fax 34 93 272 3811

diplomatic@ac-hoteles.com

Opening date: May 1999

Rooms: 211

Services: restaurant, bar, business facilities, laundry service, free coffee shop, free minibar,

1st Cafe (open 5 to 7am) 24 hr room service

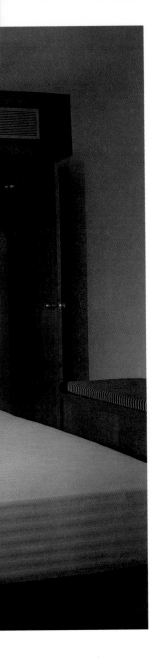

Clean lines and modern interiors make way for comfortable guestrooms that seal out the city noise and offer a free minibar, among other perks. A whitebed stacked with fluffy pillows rests against wood walls and floors. The bathroom is wrapped in exquisite green marble, equipped with all the necessary bath accessories.

Klare Linien und moderne Einrichtung zeichnen diese komfortablen Zimmer aus, die den Lärm der Stadt ausschließen und deren Minibar - neben anderen Extras - im Preis inbegriffen ist. Ein weißes Bett voller kuscheliger Kissen hebt sich von Holzwänden und –böden ab. Das Bad ist in exquisiten grünen Marmor gehüllt und mit sämtlichen Accessoires ausgestattet.

Lignes claires et intérieurs modernes ouvrent le chemin à de confortables chambres d'hôtes, isolées du brouhaha de la ville et offrant un mini bar libre, entre autres plaisirs. Un lit blanc, où s'amoncellent des coussins duveteux, s'adosse à un sol et des murs de bois. La salle de bain s'habille d'un exquis marbre vert, et est dotée de l'ensemble des accessoires nécessaires.

Hotel Aitana

Architects: GCA Arquitectos

Interior designer: Flora Rafel

Photographer: © Jordi Miralles

Owner: Cadena Ac-Hoteles

Address: Paseo de la Castellana, 152, 28046 Madrid, Spain

tel. 34 914 584 970 fax 34 914 584 971

aitana@ac-hoteles.com

Opening date: March 1999

Rooms: 112, (24 non-smoking) handicapped services

Services: restaurant, gym, laundry service, two conference rooms with audiovisual
equipment, mobile phones, translations, secretary hire, photocopier,
messenger service, travel agency, coffee shop, free press, private parking
interactive television, minibar, 24 hr room service

Hotel Portixol

Architect: Rafael Vidal

Interior designers: Johanna & Mikael Landström, Christian Aronsen

Photographer: © Helen Pie, © Stellam Hierner

Owners: Johanna Landström and Mikael Landström

Address: Sirena, 27, 07006 Palma de Mallorca, Spain

tel. 34 971 271 800   fax 34 971 275 025

www.portixol.com

hotel@portixol.com

Original construction: 1954

Opening date: 1999

Rooms: 24 (11 non-smoking)

Services: bar, restaurant, banquet and convention room, swimming pool, solarium

The Prince of Wales

Architect: Alan Powell

Interior designer: Paul Hecker

Photographer: © Earl Carter

Owners: John & Frank van Haandel

Address: St. Kilda Beach, St. Kilda, Melbourne, 3182, Australia

tel. 61 3 95 36 1111   fax 61 3 95 36 1100

www.theprince.com.au/hotel.htm

thedesk@theprince.com.au

Original construction: 1934

Opening date: September 1999

Rooms: 40

Services: bar, Circa restaurant, café Circ, wine shop, parking, high tech audivisual equipment

Kirketon

Architects: Burley Katon Halliday Architects

Photographer: © Sharin Rees

Original construction: 1930's

Address: 229 Darlinghurst Rd., Darlinghurst NSW, 2010 Sydney, Australia

tel. 61 2 9332 2211 fax 61 2 9332 2499

www.kirketon.com.au

Opening date: 1999

Rooms: 40

Services: restaurant, bar, business facilities, secretarial services, air conditioning, minibar, parking

Design Suites

Architect: Ernesto Goransky

Photographer: © Design Suites Archive

Owner: Design Suites SA

Address: Marcelo T. de Alvear 1683, 1060 Buenos Aires, Argentina

tel./fax 54 11 4814 8700

www.designsuites.com

marketing@designsuites.com

Opening date: August 1999

Rooms: 40

Services: restaurant, gym, laundry and dry cleaners, conference room, national press,
climatized swimming pool, cable, DDI, fax modem, Internet access, minibar, espresso
machine, individual air conditioning and heating, hydromassage, safe box, room service
from 7 am to 11 pm. Free installation of computer, printer, or fax

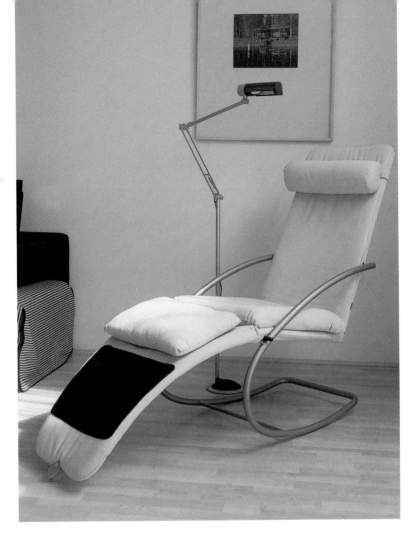

A monochrome palette of ivory, steel, and light wood coexist with minimalist furniture, generating cool and weightless interiors.

Die monochrome Farbpalette aus Elfenbein, Stahl und hellem Holz und das minimalistische Mobiliar kühle coole, schwerelose Innenräume.

Une palette monochrome d'ivoire, d'acier et de bois clair coexiste avec un mobilier minimaliste, engendrant des intérieurs sereins et légers.

Hotel Camberland

Architects: Zarr Arquitectura (Roberto Zubeldia and Ramiro Zubeldia)

Photographer: © Juan Hitters

Owner: Vía del Sol SA

Address: Ruta 8, 64,5 km, Fátima, Pilar, Buenos Aires, Argentina

tel. 54 2322 491950/499110/499111

www.camberland.com.ar

Opening date: 2000

Rooms: 20

Services: restaurant, gym, auditorium

Audacious volumes of aluminum and glass emerge from a rural terrain. Their interaction establishes the borders between public and private areas. A perimetral gallery and series of terraces communicate rooms with the exterior.

Gewagte Körper aus Aluminium und Glas wachsen aus dem ländlichen Grundstück heraus. Ihre Überschneidungen bilden die Grenzen zwischen öffentlichen und privaten Bereichen. Eine umlaufende Galerie und mehrere Terrassen verbinden die Zimmer mit draußen.

Des volumes audacieux d'aluminium et de verre émergent de la campagne. Leurs interactions établissent les limites entre les sphères privée et publique. Une galerie d'enceinte et une suite de terrasses font communiquer les pièces avec l'extérieur.

Gallery Hotel Art

Architect: Michele Bönan

Photographer: © Massimo Listri, © Licia Cappelli

Owner: Lungarno Alberghi

Address: Vicolo Dell'Oro 5, Florence, Italy

tel. 39 05527263   fax 39 055268557

www.lungarnohotels.com

gallery@lungarnohotels.com

Opening date: 1999

Rooms: 65

Services: bar, air conditioning, fax and modem lines, audiovisual equipment, library, room service, limousine rental, parking

Ca' Pisani

Architect: Roberto Luigi Canovaro

Interior designers: Roberto Luigi Canovaro, Alberto Rasa

Photographer: © Sergio Sutto

Owners: Ugo and Alberto Serandrei

Address: Dorsoduro 979/a, 30123 Venice, Italy

  tel. 39 0412401411   fax 39 0412771061

  www.capisanihotel.it

  info@capisanihotel.it

Original construction: late 14th Century

Opening date: November 2000

Rooms: 29

Services: bar La Rivista, Turkish bath, free admittal to the local gym, laundry and
  ironing service, Internet access, fax, mailing service, conference room, solarium
  jacuzzi baths, bar service

Blakes Amsterdam

Architect: Anouska Hempel

Photographer: © Pere Planells

Owner: Lady Weimberg

Adress: Keizersgracht 384, Amsterdam, 1016 GB, Netherlands

tel. 31 20 530 20 10 fax 31 20 530 20 30

www.slh.com/blakesam

hotel@blakes.nl

Original construction: 17th Century

Opening date: 1999

Rooms: 26

Services: restaurant, bar, business facilities, meeting rooms

Hotel La Bergère

Architect: Feran Thommassan

Photographer: © Pere Planells

Address: Stationstraat 40, 6221 Maastricht, Netherlands

tel./fax 31 43 328 2525

www.bergere.nl/

bergere@wxs.nl

Opening date: January 2001

Rooms: 75

Services: restaurant, bar, business facilities, phone, fax, laundry service, gift shop, parking

Dear guest,
When you don't want to be disturbed
you can mention this by hanging "her"
outside your door. This true watch-dog
will guard you and so you can enjoy your
undisturbed rest.
Les Bergères

Devi Gahr Palce

Architects: The Architectural Alliance (Gautam Bhatia and Naveen Gupta)

Interior designer: Rajiv Saini

Photographer: © Aarit Pasricha

Address: PO Box no. 144, Udaipur, 313001, Rajasthan, India

tel. 91 2953 89211   fax 91 2953 893 57

www.deviresorts.com

Opening date: 2000

Rooms: 23 suites, 7 tents

Services: restaurant, bar, business facilities, gym, health and beauty salon, swimming pool,
sports, library, museum, shops, babysitter, physician, 24 hr room service

Dramatically white and modern interiors retain just enough Indian detail to remain authentic and contemporary at the same time. These details are expressed through shapes, textures and patterns.

Die theatralisch weiße und moderne Einrichtung bewahrt gerade so viele indische Details, um authentisch und zeitgenössisch zugleich zu bleiben. Diese Details werden durch ihre Gestalt, Texturen und Muster ausgedrückt.

Des intérieurs modernes et théâtralement blancs conservent juste une touche indienne, restant à la fois authentiques et contemporains. Ces détails se révèlent par les formes, textures et motifs.

The Manor

Architects: U+A limited

Photographer: © Ram Rahman

Address: 77 Friends, Colony [West], New Dehli, 110065, India

tel. 91 11 692 5151 fax 91 11 692 2299

Opening date: May 2000

Rooms: 18

Services: restaurant, bar, gym, sauna, meeting rooms, chauffeur service,
dedicated servicing for women

This hotel´s new image is based on adding a modern twist to a classically traditional space. Rooms range from classic to contemporary. Louis Philippe antiques blend with contemporary lighting and furnishings.

Das neue Image dieses Hotels basiert darauf, daß man dem klassischen Raum einen Hauch Modernität hinzugefügt hat. Die Zimmer reichen von klassisch bis modern. Louis-Philippe-Antiquitäten harmonieren mit modernen Lampen und Möbeln.

La nouvelle image de cet hôtel repose sur l'apport d'une touche de modernisme à un espace traditionnel. Les chambres s'échelonnent du classique au contemporain. Les antiquités Louis Philippe se marient avec le mobilier et l'éclairage contemporain.

Akasaka Hotel

Architect: Kenzo Tange

Address: 1-2 Kioi-cho, chioda-ku, Tokyo, 102-8585, Japan

tel. 03 3243 1111   fax 03 3262 5163

www.princehotels.co.jp/english/

Opening date: October 1972

Rooms: 761

Services: restaurants, bars, business facilities, laundry service, minibar, dryer, video deck, voicemail

Habita Hotel

Architects: TEN Arquitectos (Bernardo Gómez Pimienta & Enrique Norten)

Photographer: © Luis Gordoa

Address: Av. Presidente Masaryk 201 Col. Polanco, C.P. 11560 Mexico, D.F.

tel. 5 282 3100   fax 5 282 310

www.hotelhabita.com/ingles/

Opening date: October 2000

Rooms: 36

Services: restaurant, bar, individual heating and air conditioning, music, minibar,
rooftop swimming pool / solarium, health spa

Das Triest

Architect: Peter Lorenz

Designer: Conran Design

Photographer: © Herbert Ypma

Original construction: 17th Century

Address: Wiedner Yampstrasse 12, 1040 Wien, Austria

tel. 43 1 589 18-0 fax 43 1 589 18-18

www.designhotels.com

back@dastriest.at

Opening date: December 1995

Rooms: 72

Services: restaurant, bar, business facilities, air conditioning, satellite, video, minibar

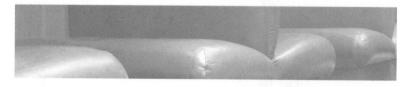

Le Méridien

Architect: Jean Hughes Tricart

Interior designer: Didier Lefort

Photographer: © Tim Mc Kenna

Address: PO box 190, Vaitape, Bora Bora, French Polynesia

tel. 689 605151 fax 689 605152

www.lemeridien-borabora.com

sales@lemeridien-tahiti.com

Opening date: July 1998

Rooms: 100 bungalows

Services: restaurant, beach bar, activities, excursions, air conditioning, minibar

A string of 85 overwater bungalows and 15
beach bungalows scattered over 7 hectares
seemingly float atop a turquoise coral reef
that surrounds Bora Bora´s lagoon; a paradise
most people only dream of.

Eine Kette aus 85 Wasser- und 15 Strand-
Bungalows verteilt sich über 7 Hektar und
scheint auf dem türkisen Korallenriff zu
schweben, das die Lagune von Bora Bora
umgibt. Ein Paradies, von dem die meisten
nur träumen.

Une kyrielle de 85 bungalows sur pilotis et
de 15 bungalows sur la plage, clairsemés sur
7 hectares, semble flotter sur un récif de corail
turquoise qui ceint le lagon de Bora Bora; pour
beaucoup seulement un rêve paradisiaque.